Agile Leadership
A leader's guide to Orchestrating Agile Strategy, Product Quality and IT Governance

Tony Adams

iUniverse®

AGILE LEADERSHIP
A LEADER'S GUIDE TO ORCHESTRATING AGILE STRATEGY, PRODUCT QUALITY AND IT GOVERNANCE

Copyright © 2015 Tony Adams.

All rights reserved. No part of this book may be used or reproduced by any means, graphic, electronic, or mechanical, including photocopying, recording, taping or by any information storage retrieval system without the written permission of the publisher except in the case of brief quotations embodied in critical articles and reviews.

iUniverse books may be ordered through booksellers or by contacting:

iUniverse
1663 Liberty Drive
Bloomington, IN 47403
www.iuniverse.com
1-800-Authors (1-800-288-4677)

Because of the dynamic nature of the Internet, any web addresses or links contained in this book may have changed since publication and may no longer be valid. The views expressed in this work are solely those of the author and do not necessarily reflect the views of the publisher, and the publisher hereby disclaims any responsibility for them.

Any people depicted in stock imagery provided by Thinkstock are models, and such images are being used for illustrative purposes only.
Certain stock imagery © Thinkstock.

ISBN: 978-1-4917-5899-1 (sc)
ISBN: 978-1-4917-5900-4 (e)

Library of Congress Control Number: 2015901240

Printed in the United States of America.

iUniverse rev. date: 01/21/2015

Contents

Preface v
Introduction vii
Acknowledgements ix
Why Agile? Why we even need Agile? Discussions around the
    Agile manifesto 1
Business goals and objectives 3
People and process adaptation 4
What is Agile and important terminologies: Putting Agile to work 5
The Scrum: The Sprint cycle: Program and Portfolio level 8
Epics and User stories 9
Release Planning 10
Agile Delivery 11
    Envision 11
    Speculate 12
    Explore 13
    Adapt and Close 16
Agile Quality Assurance for better product 18
Agile leadership from Program and Projects perspectives 22
IT Governance 25
The Agile Leadership factor: How to harness agility while being
    successful in IT Governance and in leading a TCoE (Testing
    center of excellence) 32

IT Strategy and IT Budget 38
A Case Study: The guiding principles for setting agile in motion,
    putting processes in place, building the team culture and
    putting governance in place 43
Summary 49

Preface

As more and more IT organizations are embracing Agile to deliver products and service offerings to customers, the challenges remain on some key questions. How do I better manage by product backlog? How do I run parallel overlapping sprints and effectively manage depended stories cross sprints? How do I better plan release processes? How IT can deliver business value in a most effective way while managing change control and while good governance is in place? How micro and macro level business and IT delivery frameworks can harmonize so that they make sense in enterprise level? How quality assurance can mesh into the true agile value circle so that quality of the product meets business's expectations? We will take a deeper dive into these challenging topics.

Introduction

Architecting and Orchestrating Agile focuses not only on the day to day agile activities and people interaction, but also focuses on the designing aspects of Agile. And it starts with Program and Portfolio stakeholders' alignment of strategic themes, driving clarity with business and architectural Epics and how that fits down to program level tactical planning. The leadership must make sure that the technology team understand the business value of a product feature and do anything possible to keep the development cost down. And at the same time, the business and product owners should understand the technology that help them to function better and solve business problems effectively. This emergence is a true gain for an agile organization.

In this book, we will look into some foundational aspects of Agile and then take a deeper dive into how to design, develop and nurture a successful agile organization with emphasis on quality assurance and governance in addition to the agile framework.

Acknowledgements

Special thanks to my daughter, Meghan Adams, who encourages me every day to process things calmly, drive solutions in a positive way and have a positive outlook in life.

Why Agile? Why we even need Agile? Discussions around the Agile manifesto

Agile is a philosophical foundation for effective and efficient software development. The whole point is that agile allows us to build a system or a product iteratively. For example, let's not complete the whole house before we move in rather, build section by section and once each section is complete, we can live in those completed sections. The Agile manifesto deals with Individuals and interactions over processes and tools, working software over comprehensive documentation, Customer collaboration over contract negotiation, responding to change over following a plan. While there is value in the items on the right, we value the items on the left more.

The focus of Agile is to ensure that we gain customer satisfaction by rapid, continuous delivery of useful software. When Agile is implemented, it is important that a working software is delivered frequently. A good thing about Agile is that the working software is the principal measure of progress. As long as what we are implementing are working as desired, then Agile is a successful framework for that organization. The advantage of Agile is that even late changes in requirements are not an out of norm and usually manageable. The most important factor to ensure you are agiling is by connecting closely between business people and developers on a daily basis. I should

Tony Adams

mention that nothing is more effective than face to face conversation if possible. But we live in a very distributed work environment these days, thus, video conference, or phone conferences at minimal, are also good way of ensuring that people are connected and are talking. Since Agile is a team coordinated and collaborated dynamic process, it is imperative that continuous attention is given to technical excellence and good design. Agile motto is to have the flexibility to adapt to changing circumstances.

Business goals and objectives

The ultimate responsible people who sets the business goals and objectives are the existing managers, leaders, and executives. Those business goals and objectives are typically cross-cutting customer facing initiatives that are transformed into business epics. An organization must have a clear understanding of its business goals and objectives for short and long terms. The more clarity an organization have on their business goals, the higher the efficiency level it achieves in terms of backlogging and delivering the business epics. What drives quality of the product should also be at the center of the conversation. Thus, putting an extra emphasis on quality assurance on the whole spectrum from user stories to post release smoke testing. The product owners, business thinkers of the organization help the entire organization by explaining the goals and objectives which will help generate and increase revenue, drive efficiencies, cut costs and most importantly drive customer satisfactions. A cohesive IT governance can bring IT and business closer to understand cost savings rather than IT and business debating about what IT could solve and what it would cost. Good governance is about superior results on IT investments.

People and process adaptation

The Agile Team is empowered to elaborate, prioritize, design, build and test must be part of an adaptable team – a team that is ready to change and adapt changing needs of the business. A continuous learning and adapting culture is very critical to deliver value for the customer and the business. A true agile organization is in a highly interacting, growing, helping, sharing and learning environment. Creating an agile eco system where business is feeling the value and technologists feel that they are contributing to the business by delivering cost efficiently. The sense of budget savings when it comes to delivery efficiency adds true value across organization. The business understands and participates in ensuring the quality of the product while agile quality assurance and testing processes are executed. The technology understand the product so well that they provide insights to the product owners and managers to create an even better product. The leadership challenge has been around creating and fostering that level of ownership and partnership integration and create a harmonious agile eco system.

What is Agile and important terminologies: Putting Agile to work

In an agile environment, there are some terminologies that are frequently used. Having a clear understanding of these terminologies provides the Agile team a better and effective understanding of processes and expectations from each other.

Agile Manifesto deals with the whole concept of being flexible, more collaboration with customers. We touched on this before. Agile is a lean software development process within which Kanban, a tool, resulted from lean manufacturing, embraces concepts of "task board," "work in progress" and sprint. You will also hear about the Sprint Planning Meeting which allows the team to discuss two important items. One is the meeting with product manager(s) to have a better understanding of the product itself and the second important item in the Sprint Planning Meeting is discussions around how the product needs to be built. The product manager(s) needs to be present in both sessions. Cross-Functional Team takes advantage of this meeting to clarify Nitti gritty items. In agile, product owner adds value by identifying unit of requirement which could be estimated, planned, developed and tested and called User Story. A very large user story is usually called Epic. It is a general practice to create an Epic sometimes where the plan is to break down into smaller stories later and some or all of the future user stories are perhaps still unknown. Sprint is an iteration process in which user stories are defined, designed, tested and delivered. Before each sprint, there is sprint planning meeting. This meeting allows the team to recognize user stories and help prioritize them. In addition, in this meeting, real and material plans are put together to deliver those user stories. Product backlog is review in this meeting by product owners. They elaborate what needs to be built and what the expectations are. The team elaborates the user stories and breaks them down to tasks and delivery units. This is time estimation should be done too. A well-coordinated agile team should be comfortable with a working framework to pull user stories from a product backlog into a sprint backlog to break down the features into tasks. The daily standup meeting allows the team to inform each other the status of their work and potential challenges. While all these happening, backlog grooming allows agile team to continue to add new user stories to the backlog, prioritize existing user stories if needed, prepare estimates and break down epics or larger stories into smaller stories or tasks. Retrospective allows the team to identify anything that did not go as intended in the last sprint and plan for continuous improvement. Perhaps, identify few high priority items and improve those. It is prudent to put emphasis on VOC which is Voice of Customer. It allows the entire team to understand what the customers like and/or dislike with features that have been delivered. A burndown chart helps the team to understand how much work is left across time. This is actually a very important tool for the sprint team as on one end they can see the work left for a specific period and also the work that has been completed and no longer on the "to do" list.

The fundamental difference between Agile and Waterfall is that waterfall is a sequential software development process. The key here is that waterfall is more predictable whereas agile's advantage is its adaptability. Agile team enjoys to change and adaptation flexibility. Agile's success is measured by "working software."

We all have been in situations where a lot times we face long software development cycles, changing priorities that interferes with what we had planned on and often our final products fail to meet the expectations of the customers. That is where the concept of Hybrid Agile-Waterfall software development has been tested in many organizations. Waterfall gives that certainty of expectations whereas agile gives that adaptability.

The Scrum: The Sprint cycle: Program and Portfolio level

The leadership team must have a skin the game in terms of designing the business strategy which meshes well with the business-technology process framework. The lean agile leaders should be engaged to ensure the portfolio vision is elaborated adequately to the agile teams in team levels. The intermediary program level teams like product management, business owners, and release management must define and elaborate the program objective and goals to the sprint level teams. There must be a handshake between these two teams so that portfolio and program level business goals are well understood by the sprint team. The scrum allows agile way of managing projects. The scrum relies heavily on self-organization and cross functional team efforts. What guides this is the understanding that the cross functional team will solve the problems and address the opportunities by itself. The issues are identified by the team and solved by the team. The leadership should have two key roles for the scrum process. The scrum master is the coach who will facilitate the interaction of the team in addressing the issues and resolving them. She or he helps the team perform at the highest level. At the portfolio level, always remember to take a look at the product backlog or even in strategy sessions on what makes economic and financial sense. Take consideration of the cost associated with "delaying a feature" or "not taking account for an opportunity now."

Epics and User stories

Epic owners who own business epics and architectural epics work as lean agile leaders to ensure that portfolio level epics are well understood and added to program epic backlog. Many times Epics are defined program or team level and viewed only was a "large user story." Some of the epics must be addressed in the portfolio level as they warrant detailed analysis and may have substantial impact to ROI. These portfolio level epics impact cross organizations and span out multiple releases. Portfolio management works closely with product management in program level and with product owners in team level to ensure that business epics are well translated into features. Agile teams comprised of scrum master, product owners, developers and testers work closely to understand program level backlogs and get organized with team level backlogs. The team backlog consists of everything all inclusive list of things that needs to be done.

Release Planning

All the communications and interactions that we learned about between the portfolio, program and team level can be further solidified via release planning process. This process allows development teams to be in sync with business owners. The release planning process happens to meet the project and program goals via planning and execution of the agile iterations. Part of the planning is to ensure cross teams and cross programs are being connected and efforts are synergistic. Release planning is a great vehicle to share business plan, roadmap, what features are expected to support the business.

Agile Delivery

Envision

The business owners and business strategy owners will have an edge if they can better foresee the dynamics of the business and changing priorities. The clearer they are in understanding the products that would support the business's roadmap and vision, the more effective and efficient agile process will be. The business stakeholders have a big responsibility to guide the rest of the organization to better understand that the product that would be built would look like. This phase can also be beneficial for agile leaders to ensure product requirements are formulated to fit the current business needs and new or upcoming business opportunities. Market place changes and problems with existing solutions should influence the envisioning work that happens during this phase. The product owners must lay out very clear vision and concept of the product so that the rest of the team doesn't have to spend too much time exploring scope of time product. The leadership team must encourage product owners to provide effective product vision guidance to the rest of the organization to ensure the "exploration" cost is minimal. In this phase, it is also prudent to look into the Product architecture at this stage as not visioning the architecture may turn out to be costly at later phase. This has a significant impact to the agile initiatives that may require 3rd party vendor assistance, outsourcing, distributed development, partnering with other software companies. The key note here is that in traditional understanding, architecture is referred to as scoping of a design and be as much definitive as possible, but in agile, architecture is an ongoing guide to product design and development.

Speculate

This is almost an extended version of the envision phase where the team tries to get more elaborate answers to the product(s) to be designed. The leadership would want to ensure that the team is engaging in broad discussions around the features and requirements of the product(s). Design and implementation conversations could also take place in this phase. Through these detailed dialogs and conversations, the program and portfolio management can help build the product backlog better with less dubious stories. This phase a great place to look into budget and cost aspects of requirements, design, infrastructure and ownership of the product. Putting together a flexible and adaptable plan can embrace change and changing requirements by product owners. As agile, by design, a highly adaptable model, speculating process is more appropriate in this fluid framework over "planning." As we move forward, we speculate and we adapt to changing needs of the product and project. Which brings up a relevant concept of "wrong planning." We avoid wrong planning by speculating the release plan. Our end goal is to be able to create a product structure that is elaborated by features that are well understood between product teams and architecture and technical teams. The team collectively review each feature and the technical team assess tasks at hand and estimates them. This framework allows full transparency between product managers and technical teams. If there is a time crunch, the product manager cannot request to adjust testing time, she can only request to pull out feature X. Similarly, the technical team cannot just add a feature or enhance a feature because it would be "cool." The product owner must approve it. As you can see, the speculation phase helps agile teams to better understand the evolution of features, better design adaptation of unfolding project, better prioritize the highest value features and adjust to trade-offs.

Explore

Once the envisioning and speculating phases are solidified, the agile team needs to explore. Part of exploration is getting organized as a team to execute on the plan. The key point to remember that the leadership-partnership style management reinforces the essence of agile, an innovating, emergent culture. The success of explore would remain on how collaborative the team is, how team is molding, how each team member's capabilities are supporting rest of the team, how well the road blocks are being removed. Bottom line is that the orchestration of interactions of the team should generate optimal performances. Agile discipline allows and encourages that the team manages itself. Meaning each member understands her/his responsibilities and workload. Through this practice, the team members work successfully through the iterations. The coaches need to monitor the performance outcomes to ensure that each team member is motivated and being able to achieve his or her goals.

The team should be able to anticipate the changes and the design that would help deliver maximum features smoothly. If you think about it, less adaptation requirement may be a good thing as there anticipated design didn't deviate much. The agile process is flexible enough to allow some degree of experimentation. The agile leaders must keep in mind that experimenting should have clear goals around achieving cost efficiency or improved quality. Experimenting should have focus on customer value and simple design to avoid non-essential. In an agile environment, the team always focuses on continuous improvement of the product. A better product is one that meets customer needs and deliver values today and also be flexible enough for the future to add value for the customer. One key note that in this phase, it is prudent to think about the product in a way so that the internal intricacies of the product is flexible despite external features may be less flexible. So when future feature requests come from customer, it is easier to adapt and deliver enhancement. So anytime we are designing a product, we must test it thoroughly and again, when we are enhancing the product features, a thorough testing needs to happen so that the existing product features are fully functional. A healthy debate would be why we keep making the product more flexible when it is already working. The answer is that the existing product is gradually becoming rigid and require that level of continuous improvement which is cheaper proposition than a big bang upgrade. The Agile leadership team must have a good pulse on the team interactions and communications. The Agile PM should be successful in molding each agile team member into the agile team. The smooth orchestration by agile PM of the agile interactions, activities, iterations, communication and collaboration is the key to a vibrant and successful agile organization.

Decision making collaboratively gives each team member a feeling of ownership. The key here is that via discussions, dialog, debate, at the end, a decision needs to be made. The team must not get stuck inside processes etc., rather make decisions on the information at hand. A supportive culture of decision making helps avoid too many contradicting decisions. That is why, decision framing is a key as it helps the team to identify who makes what decisions and who owns what decisions. Also the team needs to look into who should have an input and who is impacted by a decision. In agile, decisions are often made in all levels of the organization, thus, the decision framing can drive clarity in the decision making process. Just because decisions are being made in all levels, make no mistake that the portfolio and program level decisions are made by visionary leaders from both product and architecture sides.

Adapt and Close

The leadership team along with the product owners and architectural epic owners must have a really good feedback process in place so that product quality, product functionality and performance, team performance and individual goals all are shared and program or sprint level retrospect are successful. A culture must be fostered where the team can always ask if the customers receiving the intended value, if the technology team getting the support they need to produce quality and high performance product, if the iterations smooth enough and finally, if the adaptability within teams is in comfortable level.

Establishing a customer focus group helps the entire organization understand if they are adapting and managing the feedback process in alignment with strategic business goals. This is critical in many level. It helps the organization establish a leadership team that takes ownership of the customer experiences and product requirements. Even though it is customary to engage focus group at the end of each sprint or major release, it is recommended that this team is engaged when we are on envision phase. A recurring meeting with leadership and customer leaders is always beneficial to set the stage of a collaborative culture. Even though there are senior representatives working closely with the agile team to elaborate product features, it always helps to have a bigger group to help understand expectations around usability, navigation, performance etc. After each of the focus group sessions, the product owners and technical teams should capture the ideas, requests and plug that into the product design considerations, thus, making it a true flexible and adaptable environment. We must remember that the right level of customer focus group participation along with right level of technical review is the key to keep the cost of iteration low. And that's the opportunity for leadership to design a high performing agile organization. In closing, retrospective is key to understand what went right and what went wrong during all the phases.

Agile Quality Assurance for better product

Quality Assurance in agile organization is driven by same philosophy which is quality and continuous improvement. By working closely with the product managers, the agile development team ensures that product features work as they should be and defects are removed post testing. The best way to measure that quality assurance processes are working is to measure how well the products are working as they are supposed to. The agile leadership should plan quality while Epics are being designed at the portfolio level. The question becomes how to build quality as part of user story design and not as an inspection task. The agile leadership's goal is to focus on highest product quality is considered while product owners are defining epics and user stories. One thing agile team should discuss about the grade of the product versus the quality. Grade deals with product features, for example, high grade product gives you options and more features whereas low grade product gives less features. However, quality always takes precedence over grade of the product. Agile is a great framework for team to take quality into level 5 in the CMMI [Capability Maturity Model Integration] levels. Level 5 is a standard that describes an organization that relies on innovative and qualitative measurements not only to deliver the product features but also to continually improve the product. And that is comparatively easier to attain in an agile organization as teams are focused on continuous improvement. So the Agile leadership must ensure that the agile team is working well with right skills. They should foster a rapid learning and training environment. So the key question becomes, how to balance a self-governing and high performing agile team with CMMI and Governance that are sometimes focused with external (external to agile team) audits. So here again, the leadership needs to understand what is the adequate level of CMMI adoption to measure and deliver quality in agile framework. To build and maintain an effective agile quality assurance practice, the leadership should always ask some of the following questions:

1. How well the agile tester are working with the rest of the team?
2. How could the team stay engaged in quality despite wearing a different role?
3. Do we have good measurement matrix in place?
4. How do we manage a team and work that may be distributed across the globe?

It is paramount to have a defect logging, tracking and resolution process in place so that we can have metrics. If an organization is transitioning to short iterations of agile, then the cultural change should be compensated with training and process improvements. Agile testing is advantageous in a sense that the whole testing process does not get squished at the end of development phase from traditional development perspective rather it is due to the incremental and iterative nature of the agile development, testers get involved in incremental code testing. The story is not "done" until it has been tested. So from agile leadership standpoint, the more the testers are meshed into the requirements and development process, the better their understanding would be on what the business wants. While the portfolio and program level business and architectural epics are being defined and designed, a comprehensive quality management plan should be created. This would help the agile team to understand quality metrics and process improvement plans.

From Quality standpoint, the agile manifesto encourages individual interactions, working software, customer partnership and being ready to respond to change and all these are at the core of true agile testing. When it comes to quality, the whole team is responsible. So the key here is that the agile leadership should focus on the "agile testing mindset" which is to have the team focus on business value, result driven, and collaboration. So it is important to set the agile team attitude on positive "let's help each other" mindset before bringing in any changes. Agile test culture is all about whole organization is responsible for quality and testers are not just "test cops." So it is important to have representation from quality assurance team in leadership conversation in portfolio and program level while business and architectural epics are being discussed. Sometimes there is misconception about metric documentation as "not so agile" but in reality metrics help team understand how on track it is on. The whole agile team should be able to utilize defect tracking processes and tools.

The agile team should be able to identify the problems and solution sets and leadership should support that culture and framework rather than someone telling the team what to do when it comes to quality. The agile test team can play a critical role by demonstration scenarios and workflows to the agile leadership and to the bigger agile team in an iterative environment. As part of the sprint planning, security, performance, scalability, stress and load testing should be well planned. The agile team should consider keeping the customer involved in all types of testing. A good reporting mechanism to share test results with agile leadership helps them to see where the quality stands. This helps to apply continuous improvement of the product. Remember, the customer will feel that the product features meet their expectation and desired behavior when each of the user stories are well illustrated.

Agile leadership from Program and Projects perspectives

The program management team assists the leadership team by defining and designing programs and projects which supports their strategy and ROI plans. The leadership team is usually comprises of Business managers who oversee and own various parts of the business like sales, marketing, finance, operations, products, technology etc. They work collaboratively to drive the organizational objectives. The opportunity here is to ensure that program and project management successfully molds with rest of the organization to harmonize the agile framework. Every successful customer focus company sets clear strategic goals. Agile portfolio managers and leaders should be able to take each business goal and dissect into measurable unit of requirements or at least a theme. This process is crucial to create the portfolio level backlog. Once these strategic themes are well define and translated into smaller unit requirements or themes, they can all go into the backlog as epics or user stories. It is not expected that these are absolute unit level user stories that the sprint team would utilize. But rather these user stories and epics capture the business strategies and vision of the organization. The business and technology leaders take ownership of this backlog. The key is to be able to define the strategic goals of the organizations and allocate budget appropriately. These day and age, market changes rapidly and competitors are very aggressive.

A company's business drivers need to be short and long term and be very in depth so that it can withstand all these dynamic market forces and changes. So the budget must take into account what creates the company's unique aptitude. It is critical that portfolio budgeting takes account of the market challenges and opportunities. For example, if a company is acquiring smaller companies, then standardizing various systems platforms to bring users in one platform and software would create significant cost savings and improved customer experiences. Such product creation and improvement is part of a portfolio budget strategy. This strategy is tested with solid decision gates. The key question the business leaders ask are whether creation of new products and services, or enhancing existing ones are complementing the vision and values. These vision and values help create business cases that justifies the epics and user stories for the portfolio backlog.

Transitioning to more on the tactical side of agile, more clarity in business and strategy goals result in stronger business cases encapsulated with clear requirements. Which brings up the release planning and vision. How to orchestrate these epics and user stories in portfolio level and organize and size in a way so that the agile team understands the requirements is critical. Processes must be put in place so that this level of collaboration is done. Architectural epic must be developed at this level so that the enterprise level framework complements the efforts designing and developing product level features. So on one end, the business leaders brainstorm new business opportunities, cost savings, qualitative gains from customer experiences improvements, changes in the market places, opportunities to improve or enhance current processes and systems and on the other end epic owners take those ideas and information and transform them into epics and stories. Synchronization of all these stories that holistically create a product or a subset of features must be done with a lot of thoughts, insights and collaboration. It is sometimes difficult but critical to vision the pieces that need to be orchestrated in certain order. So the user stories within a sprint and in some cases, in parallel or subsequent sprint(s) needs to be well thought through. For example, if a product needs a platform to run, a certain features of the platform needs to be developing while the product is being designed developed so that product could be tested on the platform at optimal a point. The agile leadership team in conjunction with the portfolio and project level lean agile leaders must apply their combined expertise in architecture and product DNA to vision this type of sequencing. It requires collaboration and in depth design discussion prior to designing the sprint backlog. That is where the real value work is for the release management, product management and agile teams to really dissect the stories and find the common threads.

IT Governance

Process, Artifacts and people: Three key elements of agile governance. The leadership team must work collaboratively across organizations to formulate processes and structures so that all the epics and user stories that come from all corners of the organization are well justified from ROI or qualitative gain perspectives. Point is, every idea is not a revenue generating idea. Some are revenue killers or have potential to negatively impact the customer. That's why the review gates are critical. This process synergizes with the prioritization process that we talked about earlier. A successful agile organization must have their processes and artifacts well defined. The user story template, the prioritization process, the idea to user story process etc. are some great example of artifacts. A matured organization is good in base lining these artifacts and periodically it reviews processes and make improvements. Clarity in role helps avoid ambiguity on who owns what processes. All the process and artifacts provides leadership team power to audit an organization. A product development is more than just product owner and tech team working together. It takes all facets of the organization to get involved in decisions, exchange information effectively, work collaboratively and own processes to ensure successful continuous releases. The Agile governance processes need to be implemented across the organization and not just in certain departments or in certain projects. Agile governance's success remains on how the agile leadership and agile team designs and architects all the processes, decision gates, delivery requirements, check points and how all these confluence together to formulate organization wide governance. The goal of good governance is to ensure the requirements that helps the business run and grow and meet customer needs are well supported via the systems the agile team is delivering. Governance ensures that framework is in place to allow the leadership to make decisions.

Effective IT governance in an agile organization addresses three questions:

1. Effective management and use of IT: What decisions should we make?
2. Who in the leadership team owns what decisions?
3. What is the process to make decisions and what are checks a balances we could put in place to monitor these decisions?

In an agile environment, the leadership team in the portfolio level, while creating the portfolio backlog must address governance topics like IT principles – what is the business role of IT, IT architecture – what is the standardization and integration requirements of IT architecture, what are the enabling and shared services of IT infrastructure, what are the business needs for IT applications and lastly which initiatives to fund and what dollar amount is justified. All these questions are intertwined and decision arrangements have profound influence on the agile governance mechanism. The IT governance must gel in with the corporate governance framework. How do we do that? We must harmonize IT goals, IT governance arrangements and IT performance goals with the organizational metrics, behaviors and governance behaviors. It needs to be clear to the rest of the organization from IT, that IT has standardized the requirements and processes that helps business achieve its goals. On the IT architecture side, there needs to be standardization on how data, applications and infrastructure are organized with set of policies and technical choices to support the business goals. In an agile environment, IT infrastructure team is part of the agile team as they bring in expertise around infrastructure to support the developed new features post go live. Infrastructure team supports network, databases, servers, provisioning and management of large scale computing, shared services, printers, OS etc. In agile framework, adding new business application or enhancing features to an existing business application requires thorough understanding of change management processes which requires planning and collaborative discussions in sprint meetings. So in order to sustain architectural integrity, we need to understand architectural demands of an organization's portfolio. That is where, the portfolio level architectural epics discussions add tremendous value. An organization constantly goes through changes for advancement and business efficiency, as such, it may create complex and opposing organizational forces. IT governance helps to reconcile these opposing and competing forces from value, quality and budget perspectives. So we discussed

Agile IT principles, IT architecture, IT infrastructure, Business applications. Last but not least, IT investment and prioritization is nothing different from company's investment, the only difference is that the IT cycle and especially in an agile shop, it is lot shorter. In the portfolio level discussions, all these decision topics needs to be discussed separately and collectively as they all overlap each other.

IT investment decisions are vetted by the agile leadership team with clear understanding of business goals. The decision making and approval processes are sometimes standardized. The agile investment committee typically should determine which projects individually or a group of projects collectively provide optimal strategic benefits for the company. Those conversations and governance processes help drive the prioritization of the portfolio level backlog. Part of that decision making and approval comprises decisions on enterprise architecture and infrastructure. Injecting the Service Level Agreement [SLA] in the decision making process improves the quality of requirements and delivery framework. The agile architecture board better understands the requirements from business and present competitive proposals to "earn" the business of the business units. It is not an unusual practice for business to encourage external providers to participate the "bidding" process to deliver services and products that support business unit's strategic goals. That process creates the chargeback process, a mechanism for allocating IT costs to the business units. This creates a discipline and that is important for governance in an agile organization. Assessing the value of agile IT organization is challenging. It requires putting a structure in place so that decisions and measurements are there. Not to mention there are always non conformists. The value of governance comes from integrating various operating groups to leverage ideas and assets from each other but same time have sufficient autonomy so that each of those groups are able to meet its goals and obligations. In a successful agile organization, more leadership members are knowledgeable about the governance. And there is an awareness and more engaged team members. This awareness helps drive clearer business objectives for IT investment. The agile team has to ensure they are providing information to the agile leadership who are the owners of decision making processes. So in order to have a good governance in place for an agile shop, the following topics:

1. The portfolio management level senior leadership are capable of making solid IT governance decisions.
2. The agile leadership can design the IT architecture and processes so that it can support the business architecture.
3. Within the processes, they has to be a structured way to deal with exceptions that may cause additional costs.
4. Make better decisions and create good portfolio backlog with better understanding of infrastructure, shared services and architecture. Understand that they are all connected.

5. Create a product innovation culture and environment with business unit autonomy.

So, in order to design agile IT governance, a set of desirable behaviors needs to be implemented; for example, consistent view of customer across business units needs to be in place. An agile leadership team who is present across organization to synchronize and orchestrate multiple business units' needs should synergize the IT initiatives. The same agile leadership team comprised of business and technology leaders makes the IT principles and investment decisions. There will always be divergent and competing forces on decision making. Pick the critical few that makes the business move towards the right direction. So the big question is whether the IT governance in your agile organization is creating desirable IT behavior and helping address your opportunities. In order to make governance effective, it needs to be designed correctly. Meaning, it involves agile leadership team to review product backlog, sprint delivery, reviewing the charge back process etc. If something is broken, redesign the governance process. Transparency, information sharing, communications are key to establishing governance that ensures business and IT have synergies. IT governance require that there are owners and accountability. At the end of the day, the Agile Senior board is responsible for the governance. For a large organization, IT governance framework needs to be in enterprise level and also in organization level and even in business unit level. Usually lower level IT governance aligns with the higher level or enterprise level. It is truly desirable that business unit level IT assets are creating business values and similarly these values are across different business units and organizations. And enterprise level IT assets, principles and architecture is effectively and efficiently delivering that value with optimal cost.

The Agile Leadership factor: How to harness agility while being successful in IT Governance and in leading a TCoE (Testing center of excellence)

Every year, new technologies, markets and competitors emerge causing leaders to rethink how to adapt to the pace of change. In order to create a leadership organization who can demonstrate agility not only in the top level but also in all levels, it is important to ensure strategic and tactical goals are set properly in all levels. The leaders should be connected closely with the customers, with the products, with the core functionality of the business. The connection deepens the understanding of the business value and help steer the agile framework, design quality and manage IT governance. This helps create a continuous learning and adaptation culture. Growing leaders in all layers and levels of the organization is definitely win. A self-organizing team is at the essence of agile. And that requires leadership.

Agile leaders have the gravity and depth to handle moment of truth with end customers. Leaders understands the customer requirements, expectations, pain points etc. Product owners and managers demonstrate leadership in developing and position products that solves critical business problems, generates revenues and influences customer experiences positively. Agile leaders get rid of bureaucracy and hierarchy. Foundation of agile is an empowered team and who decides what to do to address an opportunity or to solve a problem. Hierarchy is counterproductive in this type of framework as it makes people wait on individuals instead of making decisions as a team.

In order to be successful from organization standpoint, agile leaders should consider no walls between organizations. Information should flow bi-directionally and people should interact interdepartmental level. Here is another level. How about agile team leader physically at client location or at sister company and interacting, collaborating and brining fresh ideas and opportunities to the agile team back in the office? Observing quality of the software that client is using and understanding their quality requirements helps the agile leaders to quantify quality of the product better.

Agile is just not a way of managing an organization's software development methodology. It is broader than that. In order to make sure the agile team is successful, the business units also need to understand their processes etc. Even though agile is an environment where we are constantly learning and improving, there must be productivity goals that could be set. Agile leaders, while focusing on the business value and "working software" that solves customer's problems or creates innovation, also work closely with business to help them go through the processes that would make them better candidates to take advantage from the agile relationship. That may go all the way to restructuring of a business. Reengineering business processes and revisiting operational.

Another important component of agile leadership process is to make sure that agile leaders are not only leading in setting strategy but also good in managing well too. Too many agile organizations fails as there are too much emphasis on strategy level but not well thought out tactical planning. Agile leaders understands the IT structures, processes that help make the IT decisions which help design the IT Governance. Agile creates efficiency in IT organization and efficiency increases IT governance maturity.

Great IT leaders knows how to manage IT organization and structure it the right way and put mechanics in place that allows IT initiatives to be prioritized. Agile leadership requires cost effectiveness of IT utilization, using IT for growth and most importantly, effective use of IT for business agility.

A good agile leadership trait of an agile organization is where leaders are created, cultivated and people and talent innovation is evident in individual performance. Agile leaders help individuals to grow continuously and not encourage to bring new ideas. The Ideas that trigger positive change. But in order to foster structured change and create innovative organization, IT processes, roles and responsibilities, and quality management needs to be well understood and well defined, which helps improve IT governance performance. At the same time, agile leadership must device a continuous agile delivery across structural and architectural quality factors of the software. That quality delivery framework must check everything from security, robustness and performance in addition to functional aspects of the product. Compound all that with applications running in cloud. So agile leaders must design a fast paced, multifaceted testing environment that can keep up with a face paced agile software releases. So automation comes very handy in an agile testing organization. The right level of scale in a continuous integration environment is crucial to ensure that software quality is not compromised. A true leadership comes from simplicity and agility while a good IT decision making and governing process is in place. Leadership welcomes change and work as an enabler to focus on what is next. Leaders keep their eyes on the value for the business. Focus on what makes sense for the business and for the customers' expectation. Quality really becomes a very high priority topic as it raises the bar for the organization and for the product features. And in order to achieve that level of synergy with change and quality, process and project boundaries come into play where roles and responsibilities are well defined but the team takes ownership. Team provided feedback where feedbacks are constructive and members are supportive of each other. Even though agile is an iterative model, some form of structure is required to measure decisions and value that is the output of the team efforts. So the improvement that is learned in one iteration should converge into the second and other parallel or subsequent iterations. And with that structure and agility, true efficiency is gained. It takes leadership to design a framework to that level. Agile leaders keep improving the processes until they are fully satisfied.

At the core of building a TCoE, testing center of excellence, is defining and understanding business requirements. The leadership must synergize agile vision and test architectural vision. Agile leaders create standardization across sprints and iteration so that testing processes are simplistic and easy to repeat and leverage. And it requires an agile test talent pool that acquire and capture knowledge across different business verticals and business processes. So for enterprise level testing success, epic and user story discussions in senior leadership level helps the testing visionaries to vision the organization and planning of people and process to not only sustain but also to harness the fast paced agile cycle. The point is, these agile leaders with specific and sometimes shared ownerships must create an environment that is continuously discovering business opportunities that maximizes enterprise assets and adds value. The TCoE multifaceted services must provide the agile leaders including product owners and product managers a comprehensive look at the tools, processes and mechanics of testing. It is of interest to the technology leaders to keep the business partners aware of the testing capabilities so that business understands its strengths and maybe harmonize the pace they want the features to be deployed while optimal quality is being measured. When the business comes to TCoE and expresses their ideas and requests advice from

TCoE around ensuring highest quality standard for its products, that level of trust and partnership approach is healthy and reflection of a matured TCoE organization. The partnership for quality is embedded in how business and IT establishes each other's expectations and how collaboratively they harness the people, processes and tools to continuously raise the quality standards. Ask the business if they are satisfied with the TCoE standards. If not, what needs to happen and how much technology agile leaders can improve without asking for more time or more money. Does it make sense to invest a little more time and little more money to gain added quality value? Could the leaders quantify that value? These are some of the key conversations that both product owners and agile development leaders must have recurringly.

IT Strategy and IT Budget

The underlying need for IT differs in organizations and different industry verticals. The IT strategy for an ecommerce company is not similar to a utility company. For example, the IT strategy for amazon or ebay not similar to that of a power grid company in west coast. IT strategy and budgetary policy is different for Tiffany and United Airlines. Agile leaders constantly think about their IT strategy to ensure IT is in alignment with business strategy of the company. Agile leaders must ensure that knowledge gap is minimal within the organization. By eliminating the knowledge gap, an organization can operate more efficiently and help cut or avoid costs that does not add value to the business. In order to set effective and meaningful IT strategy, leaders should consider designing and architecting an IT organization where IT organizational function, IT architecture and agile development framework are converging well. Another component plays a significant role here which is outsourcing. Agile organization's decentralized functions along with deeper understanding of applications, software and hardware architecture is advantageous before allocating budget for outsourcing for the agile software development. One way to control IT budget is to ensure IT decisions are business demand driven while demands are well vetted and controlled. Ensure which demands and ideas are quantifiable in terms of value, revenue, efficiency and quality. But at the same time, IT leaders must ensure that every business demand does not become a contentious negotiation between IT and business. Labor and technology costs are usually most costly items in the IT budget. So architectural epics have to be smartly designed to develop an enterprise wide technology framework which streamlines and standardizes software development processes and labor costs associated with the agile iterations, sprints etc. Also when IT budgets are well planned and allocated to ensure better quality, the cost of ownership of the product is optimal. It is absolutely important for agile leadership to establish performance targets so that budget allocation could be measured. We discussed earlier that organizational leaders should have less walls between inter departments so that the information may flow fully. The knowledge flow among inter teams creates a more favorable environment for prudent IT budget decisions. The agile leaders should not only work closely with the business leaders who deal with the customer facing opportunities and issues of the company, they should have a clear idea about the company's competitors, customers, suppliers and innovation potentials. The agile leadership also work closely with business leaders across organization to understand how IT budget decisions are contributing directly to the business profitability now and in near future. Sometimes company's products competes with competitor's products in different markets. To maintain a competitive edge for the products, agile leaders must partner with product owners and leaders to help them design innovative products. So IT budget must consider that forward looking product design and architecture development to continuously support the dynamics of the business. The agile leadership must be able to "reinvent" the technology platform and be an enabler to business while investing in strategic IT projects.

The IT strategy must enable the IT organization to stay agile to address company's changing needs. IT usually does not understand the budgeting process and finance on the other hand, does not understand the technology. So inherently, there is a gap that needs to be bridged. The business leaders who work closely with the IT leadership actually can help narrow that gap. One successful approach is to baseline the structures, framework, development and testing processes along with release management processes for the strategic projects and initiatives. And build a more robust and comprehensive problem solving tasks from the baseline on each of those practices. An agile leader's role is to encourage team members to bring in solutions to the table for the roadblocks they think may happen in near or long term future. That level of trust and cultural awareness always is fruitful as it takes away the water cooler noise and promotes a solid mechanism for agile team members to bring in solutions and people start to recognize that positive management approach and attitude in people.

In agile environment, agile leadership requires agility in leading a business where uncertainty maybe the norm, where there are competing needs and priorities. Agile leader must scan the environment, understand what is working well and what is not working so well, what areas require more attention, quickly leverage subject matter experts to build new or enhance existing processes that can create a successful agile prototype framework. The agile leader must engage in understanding stakeholders' agility. What it means is to understand what the priorities for the stakeholders are. Create a common thread of understanding and language so the stakeholder's frame of reference and vision could be interpreted well. Here comes the creative part of an agile leader. Transforming the challenges and complex problems into common desired results is a higher level skill that allows agile leaders to be more effective. They begin to orchestrate problem solving with agile best practices while business leaders starts to find agile leaders working shoulder to shoulder with them in the front lines. The agile leadership may happen in different levels. Some leaders work on tactical level, solving day to day items and within their own units. They add tremendous values in terms of leading their teams and providing individual level guidance. Some leaders are now ready to tackle more on the strategic side. These agile leaders meet periodically with business leaders and share software, hardware, infrastructure challenges. The catalyst agile leaders are the transformational ones. They bring innovation to forefront, empower right people, build consensus on divergent topics and work as a catalyst for organizational changes. On the other hand, agile team members have a different styles, different way of thinking and doing things, in spite of those traits, agile team members and leaders could be very successful in different stages and different levels of agile. Most organizations are entrenched in tactical level of agile and catalyst agile leaders are sometimes focused on the tactical level to ensure "numbers are met," meaning user stories or epics are rolled out successfully. Instead, they should engage in problem solving, better governance, improving cost efficiencies, better budget allocation decisions, improving customer experiences and getting customer feedback continuously.

A Case Study:
The guiding principles for setting agile in motion, putting processes in place, building the team culture and putting governance in place

I was contacted by a specific business unit of very large corporation to help them review their newly instituted agile shop. So I showed up and had some initial conversation at the leadership level to understand what their business model was. I understood that they were intending to put agile process framework in place and just was in the learning mode on basic team level functions. Nothing very formalized as they just had several sessions. The decision was that the project would be led according to lean and agile principles. Here are some of the guiding principles the organization adopted.

We learned that the study or envision phase must not be squeezed too much which may compromise understanding of what we are trying to achieve, the vision itself and the complexity around the implementation of that vision. So we have ask ourselves a very simple question: What is the most simplistic but most valuable feature that we can easily implement which fits our long term architectural path? And keep asking the same question and move from most simplistic to more complex continuum.

Tony Adams

Our goal was to ensure that the transforming ideas into working code was achieved optimally via team interactions. One strength of the team was that each team member developed depth in knowledge in their respective areas. People, process and tools would be leveraged optimally via daily interactions. We tried our best to set boundaries clearly to avoid extra churns of "more digging into scope and newer findings." The strategy was to address new findings as they would come and plan at that point instead of trying to plan for maximum or even unknown business or technology events. The point is that the agile team should always plan for what is known today. At the same time, the team should have high confidence on the architecture or have ongoing efforts to make a good flexible and open architecture. Wrapping all these ideas and processes with defined process control principles was the key. We had sub-teams who owned the processes to enforce organizational structures. For example, within the agile sprint team, we had testing team who controlled testing, PMO experts oversaw the project and risk management, etc. We were challenged with a paradigm shift in thinking how to help technologists think on costs, budgets and benefits which designing the architecture and systems.

Our mission was clear. We were going to build a system that delivers value to our customers. Our scrum gurus put the agile development framework in place. We started to get the product managers involved in defining the backlog of user stories. Scrum and sprints were defined. Product backlog was compiled. User stories differ from traditional requirements in the sense that they don't over specify the implementation. So our user stories had just enough so that we were able to proceed to design. The agile design and development cadence helped to understand problems quickly and avoid mistakes. The agile leadership team had recurring meetings where product managers would elaborate on their product life cycle management, how that fits around marketing, sales, legal, finance etc. and on the other spectrum, technology leaders elaborated how their architecture, design, processes are in place to support product lifecycle and customer experiences. So while all these activities and interactions are happening, sprints are designed and product backlog is prioritized. One very important component to agile is the Sprint-end demo which gives the leadership team a better understanding of the status of product backlog, prioritization, adjustment needs, etc. In addition, we didn't hesitate to have more simulation of features or sub set of features. The leadership must keep in mind that while in the envision phase, while creating the portfolio backlog, constraints of business, products, legal, marketing all must be thoroughly discussed and well understood. Designing the product backlog with the constraints affect cost, timeline and quality of features heavily.

Tony Adams

All goes back to the earlier conversation we had, we kept agile principles in mind:

1. We will follow easy and continuous delivery
2. We understand the late requirements are welcome.
3. We will deliver working software as frequently as weeks or couple of months.
4. We, from all sides of business, product managers, marketing, sales, legal, back office, technology teams, all of us will work closely and if needed, daily throughout the project.
5. A working software release as frequently as possible, will be our success measurement tool.
6. We will be a fantastic self-organizing team and bring in best requirements, best design, and best architecture to deliver wow experiences for our customers.

We developed communication and reporting framework and templates. We understood that it would be lot easier for us to bring up issues and problems as they come at us and address each as needed instead of building up a problems and issues to address as a bulk.

Couple of items I would like to point out:

1. The teams should aligned with the business that they support.
2. No matter how seasoned and expert each team member is, demand and expect thorough and highest standard

documentations from respective owners. No matter how much trust and relationship is there to bank on, ensure owners of artifacts deliver what is expected of them on time. But there is a better approach. Let owners own their artifacts. For example, business owns requirements, designers own design, testers own testing and so on. What if designers and testers have input to requirements, business has input to design and testing etc? This approach is actually healthy. By all means, everyone should do testing.

3. Manage by exception is a great concept. Always take a positive approach to any deviation. Teach, guide and grow junior guys to senior level. If someone overlooked some process, help them. Foster a highly positive and interactive environment.

4. Be invested and embedded in the real development world. Don't just rely on the green, yellow and red marks on weekly report. Go see demos. Go attend meetings. Talk to testers. Talk to operations who will support the hardware, software and network post go live.

5. At last, what I mentioned earlier many times; ask "what is the minimum number of feature we could add sooner that adds value to the business?"

Summary

Agile leaders expect constant change and that is the norm. They break organizational barriers and reach out to partners, suppliers, field workers, operations, finance, people who are passionate about the product and how to market the product better. Agile leaders work as catalyst and bring changes to innovate. Every agile team member feels empowered to bring new ideas and solutions to overcome roadblocks. The Quality starts even when the ideas are being formed. TCoE (Testing Center of Excellence) design and architecture is part of that leadership initiative to continuously improve quality of the product. People, process and artifacts are key to architect effective IT Governance. IT governance must align with the corporate governance so that optimal business value could be gained. Agile leaders work closely with business and finance so that good governance results in solid decisions in budget prioritization and allocation. Understanding the pace of business and more importantly the competitors business gives the leaders an edge to align IT initiatives and be future focused. So, agile leaders must work in different levels and layers within IT and outside IT to ensure innovation is happening. Solving business problems with right projects in a collaborative manner between business and IT helps harness knowledge and builds trust. Quality should be a joint initiative between business and agile leaders. Both must take ownership of revenue generation and ultimately the customer satisfaction. Agile leadership converges business goals with right people and processes that strengthens IT capability to deliver with agility. The right vision that encapsulate quality product with processes that encourage innovation. Orchestrating all these components requires developing and maturing empowered agile leaders in all levels of the organization.

Printed in Great Britain
by Amazon